Let Us Begin

Poems of Struggle and Hope

By David Yancey

Copyright © 2025 by David Yancey

All rights reserved. No part of this book may be reproduced, stored in a retrieval system, or transmitted in any form or by any means—electronic, mechanical, photocopying, recording, or otherwise—without the prior written permission of the author, except in the case of brief quotations embodied in critical articles or reviews.

Let Us Begin: Poems of Struggle and Hope

Published by Write Side Media Group

www.writesidemediagroup.com

Cover and interior images licensed through Adobe Stock.

ISBN: 979-8-9987012-0-7

1 3 5 7 9 10 8 6 4 2

This is a work of original poetry. Names, characters, and incidents are either the product of the author's imagination or used fictitiously. Any resemblance to actual persons, living or dead, is purely coincidental.

Printed in the United States of America

First Edition

Lost
- Here I Am
- Let Us Begin
- The Space That's Empty
- I Stay

Seeking
- I Fell Short
- I Turn
- No More Alone
- The Day's Almost Over

Found
- Once in Your Life
- You Found Me
- It's Okay
- The Answer

Resolve
- The Loss of One
- An Evening Such as This
- Best Friend
- Trust the Silence

Become
- I See You
- I Can't...Let's Fly
- The Words You Told Me
- I Need

Dedication

To all who have crossed my path in this journey we call life—
whether through kindness or challenge—
thank you for inspiring me.

A Note from the Author

Beginning in 2020, after a major event in my life, these poems began to take shape—growing in number as a way to bring to life the thoughts and moments that raced through my mind, often keeping me awake at night.

This collection is a reflection of that journey. A way of naming what was once just noise in my head. Some of these poems came quickly. Others took their time. But all of them helped me move forward, even if only by an inch.

If you find something here that resonates—something you've felt but couldn't name—then maybe this is where *we* begin.

What Readers are Saying

"Dave Yancey's poems are deeply moving, raw, and incredibly heartfelt. They capture the weight of emotions—struggles with loss, faith, and self-discovery—while offering glimmers of hope and resilience.

Each piece takes the reader on a journey, whether through personal battles, the longing to be seen, or the strength found in turning to faith and love. The vulnerability in these words is powerful, making them not just relatable but profoundly meaningful.

If you've ever felt lost, uncertain, or searching for connection, these poems remind you that you are not alone—and that hope is always within reach.

A truly beautiful and inspiring collection." -- Ashley Red

"*Here I am, it resonated with me and reminded me of my darker days. However, that memory brought back what happened to allow me to move forward and beyond those dark days! David's writing hits home with every poem he writes.*"--Kevin Ferrer

"*This is not a book to tuck away. David is a romantic old soul poet who weaves powerful yet familiar emotions with a poetic finesse you won't be able to forget.*"--Cherissa McConnell

Let Us Begin   David Yancey

The Lord is near to the brokenhearted

and saves the crushed in spirit.

Psalm 34:18

Let Us Begin David Yancey

Lost

Let Us Begin

David Yancey

There are times when you want to hide,

when the pain is too much to bear—

when all you want is to be seen,

for someone to know you are there.

While *lost* may last longer than an hour or day,

hold on to the thread of hope—*found* is on the way.

Let Us Begin David Yancey

Here I am

I'm lost

I do know where I am

I have a list to do

Don't know if I can

Let Us Begin

Sitting, watching, talking, having fun
Then it hits you, why, where did it come
Tears start falling, no reason is known
Emotions raging, you feel alone

Writing, journaling, needing wanting
Praying, crying, pacing, lying
You're dying for someone to see, to know
To reach out so that you don't feel alone

Phone rings, message dings, you let it go
All strength is gone, you wish they would know
That what you need, want, pray for is a warm embrace
or somehow to just end this race

That was me then, this is me now
I cry but I don't cry alone.
I cry inside
I escape to my room

Let Us Begin

David Yancey

I just want to hide.

I open your word
I look inside
The enemy pushes harder
Telling me to hide.

I scream out, I cry out
You call my name
I run, I scatter
I hide in shame.

You touch my shoulder,
You hold my heart.
I feel your love
I know how to start.

It will be a struggle
a fight we will win.
I am not alone.
So let us begin.

The Space That's Empty

Just knowing that she was there—

the sadness lingers on.

When I look, the space is empty.

Something good is now gone.

I know this is for the better,

and I pray that friends someday we'll be.

But for now that space is empty,

and right now that's all I see.

I know I'm not lost without her.

I know I'll be alright.

I know this grief, I'll get through.

I know right now is not the night.

I Stay

So just know that
when the voices say to run
when my mind says to fade
when I just want to be done
and I can't get through this day
when everything around me says it's not worth it
when nothing else seems to matter
it's for you that I stay
It's for you I stay

As I look around me
I see all that I've done
There are so many blessings
but I focus on just one
the one that seems to be missing
and I just don't know why
to have someone to share with
this thing that we call life

Let Us Begin

David Yancey

So just know that
when the voices say to run
when my mind says to fade
when I just want to be done
and I can't get through this day
when everything around me says it's not worth it
when nothing else seems to matter
it's for you that I stay
It's for you I stay

Let Us Begin   David Yancey

Seeking

Let Us Begin

David Yancey

Unsure of where you're going—

lost is no longer home.

With each step that you take,

a direction you are choosing.

Step up—keep on moving.

Found is a day away.

I Fell Short

I fell short

Wasn't the man they needed

Wasn't the man I was meant to be

I fell short

Thought if I just focused on them it would be enough

Didn't know then what I know now

That to be what I needed to be for them

I needed to be that for me

I fell short

I'll fall short again

I am just a man doing what I need to do now

Looking to Him for direction

Looking to Him for the how

Let Us Begin

David Yancey

I fell short

I'll fall short again

I'm not looking for perfection

Not in her, not in them, not in myself, not ever again

I fell short

But the difference now I see

That because of the resurrection

Never alone will I be

I fell short

To be continued, you'll see

Let Us Begin David Yancey

I Turn

I turn to you

when there's no where else to turn

I turn to you

now when I should have turned then

I look to you for answers I do not know

I look to you for strength

I look to you to grow

I know that in you

I will find my way

I turn to you now

I turn to you today.

Let Us Begin   David Yancey

No More Alone

I'm not alone anymore
You've been with me all along
I'm not alone anymore
You've already walked through the door
And when I'm feeling scared and no where to go
I get down on my knees and know
I'm not alone anymore

Let Us Begin David Yancey

The Day's Almost Over

The days almost over,
The workday almost thru
And I am a wondering
How the hours have treated you

Some will stop and wonder
What is next for them to see
Others will start to worry
What tomorrow's going to be

For you a prayer today will show
Accomplishments and joy
For threw the trials we see
Is how our Father helps us to grow

So as your day comes to an end
And the work comes to a close
Relax and pour some wine
Enjoy this virtual rose

Let Us Begin   David Yancey

Found

Let Us Begin

David Yancey

It didn't come with thunder,

and it didn't happen overnight.

The pain—fighting to keep its hold—

but soon, you will see:

if you keep on pushing forward,

resolve will start to unfold.

Once in Your Life

Once in your life
Well for some maybe two
You meet that someone who fits
The one who's a part of you

Once in your life
You know just what to say
The words seem so right
They're not forced in any way

Once in your life
Your dreams become clear
The one that you prayed for
Has come so very near

Once in your life
Well for some maybe two
You meet someone that fits
For me that one is you

Let Us Begin — David Yancey

You Found Me

Wait...what...can you see me?

I can feel you near me.

When I look, no one's there.

Stop...no...what are you doing?

I'm scared no one will care.

Okay...yes...let's do this.

I'm glad you found me.

This path—I will dare.

Let Us Begin — David Yancey

It's Okay

I feel like you left me
when it was I who abandoned you
I feel like you don't hear me
I stopped talking, it's true

I crawl inside
I want to hide
I prayed and prayed
somehow I would just die
no more no more, I just want to cry

I hear your voice
a soft whisper in my heart
I turn towards it
I'm afraid but
I need to start

Let Us Begin
David Yancey

I'm still deep inside
filled with pain I want to hide
I pray for strength
no more no more, I want to cry

I move towards your voice
wincing with every stride
You've always been near
you never left my side

The truths which I believed
I know were just a lie
my faith in you grows stronger
with each lesson, with each trial

I'm no longer trapped inside
filled with fear, wanting to hide
Your love is the source of the strength

I always seem to find
and now I've finally learned
its okay, it's okay, you are strong, it's okay, to cry

The Answer

I've been running around in circles,

getting lost inside my mind.

I'm always looking for something,

not quite sure what I'd find.

I know the answer's out there.

I know the answer is near.

I'm looking for direction—

wanting to share what I hold dear.

My answer is found in You, God.

This I know is true.

In this I look to You now—

my heart I give to You.

Let Us Begin   David Yancey

Resolve

Let Us Begin

David Yancey

You are not who you once were,

not yet who you will be.

When pain becomes healing,

the next step is clear to see.

Keep fighting—no one can hold you back.

The strength you need is within.

Become is just before you,

You are now on the right track.

Let Us Begin — David Yancey

The Loss of One

The loss of one
Whose heart seems far
One who's meant to love you
The loss is still hard

The loss of one
You didn't really know
One who's meant to love you
A love you hoped would grow

The loss of one
You longed and dreamed to see
One who's meant to love you
Whose heart is now at peace

The loss of one
Somehow you will find
The one who's meant to love you
A love you'll know in time

Let Us Begin   David Yancey

An Evening Such as This

An evening such as this
Where two have joined in time
One filled with laughter
A joining of the minds

An evening such as this
Where two have joined in time
Both longing for each other
Their hearts now entwined

An evening such as this
Where two have joined in time
Their hands holding each other
Their prayers now their guide

An evening such as this
Where two have joined in time
What God has put together
Let no one cut the twine

Best Friend

I have enough best friends.

I'm best friend to many.

The words that cut clean through

what I want my life to be.

When you say them,

they don't land the way you think.

You call it a compliment—

but it makes me sink.

Yeah, I get it.

It's a badge I should wear.

But if I'm honest,

I don't care.

Let Us Begin
David Yancey

Okay—okay.

It's not a slight on who I am.

Just please understand:

I want more than safe someday.

I want someone who wants my hand.

So yes, I make a great best friend—

a truth I've long been told.

But if that's all you see in me,

it's not a truth I need retold.

Let Us Begin   David Yancey

Trust the Silence

Where are you?

Are you here?

I'm asking

I'm searching

I'm seeking

Am I dying?

Where are you?

Are you here?

I can't feel you

What is missing?

What aren't you answering

What am I feeling?

Where are you?

Are you here?

I'm begging

Let Us Begin

David Yancey

To hear your voice

To get an answer

To understand

It's not a choice

Where are you?

There you are

I feel your comfort

I understand

Sometimes no answer

Something so simple

Your answer is

Trust my plan

Let Us Begin   David Yancey

Become

Let Us Begin — David Yancey

As you become who you are,
it's not a sudden change.
There is still pain to unravel—new roads to unwind.
Take each step with assurance: you are not alone.
Embrace the change as it comes to shape who you
will become.

Let Us Begin David Yancey

I See You

I see you

the pain you're in

the burden you carry

the one you hide within

I see you

the love you give

to those all around you

yourself you skip

I see you

the depth in your eyes

the truths you tell others

but believe all the lies

Let Us Begin David Yancey

I see you

the pain that you see

yes, I see you...

Can you see me?

Let Us Begin   David Yancey

I Can't...Let's Fly

I can't

You must

I won't

You trust

why

Because

Not enough

Don't fuss

I stand here at the mirror

Not knowing who to believe

One side of me says push forward

The other says retreat

Let Us Begin   David Yancey

Why do you believe in me

When I know I'm not enough

Can't you see, I can't do this

I'm nothing more than dust

I can't

You must

I won't

You trust

why

Because

Not enough

Dont fuss

Let Us Begin

David Yancey

I'll try to again, once more

Maybe with you by my side

This time will be different

I'm scared I won't make it

I'm afraid not to try

Thank you, thank you

For once in my life

I believe I can do this

Let's go...let's fly

The Words You Told Me

I heard your voice speaking to me

Not in my mind

The words in my heart.

I turned around to see you

Hoping you were there

I heard your voice speaking

But you were not there

Let Us Begin

David Yancey

I heard the words you told me

Time and time again

Words that stayed with me

The wounds they would mend

I felt your love for me

A warm blanket in the night

I heard the words you told me

But you were no where in sight

And so I run into the night

Crying out your name

Not knowing where I'm going

Or if you feel the same

Let Us Begin

David Yancey

I fall to my knees ready to give in

I feel your words inside me

Your strength filling me again

I heard the words you told me

I held them in my heart

No matter where you were standing

You were with me from the start

I hold on to the words you told me

I hold them in my heart

I know where you are standing

You're with me as we start

I Need

I needed somewhere to turn

I needed somewhere to hide

I needed someone to talk to

But you were no where in sight

I needed someone to hold me

I needed somewhere to cry

I needed someone to see me

I just wanted to die

I need someone besides me

I need to walk the line

I need to stand up stronger

I need to let go of the lies

Let Us Begin

David Yancey

I have someone to turn to

I've had you all of the time

I'll stop looking behind me

I know your hand is in mine

I have all that I needed

I know its going to be alright

Let Us Begin   David Yancey

For Your Thoughts

I praise you, for I am fearfully and wonderfully

made.

Wonderful are your works;

my soul knows it very well.

Psalm 139:14

www.ingramcontent.com/pod-product-compliance
Lightning Source LLC
Chambersburg PA
CBHW030448100526
44580CB00002B/35